ENGLISH EMBROIDERY—II.

CROSS-STITCH

XVII. (29)

XVIII.(30)

v. (6)

XVIII.(32)

SAMPLER belonging to Mrs. Longman, worked by E. R. Although it has two alphabets, it is, unfortunately, undated. It is probably, however, seventeenth century, as it contains the same designs and is worked in the same silks and colours as many of the dated ones. It shows very clearly the use of the English diagonal cross-stitch with a bar and English long-legged cross-stitch with a bar, and the thickness of effect that they give.

The figures at the sides indicate references to Plates illustrating diagrams to show practical method of working.

ENGLISH EMBROIDERY—II.

CROSS - STITCH

A Handbook with Diagrams, Scale Drawings
and Photographs taken from XVIIth Century
English Samplers and from Modern Examples

By

LOUISA F. PESEL

Author of " Practical Canvas Embroidery " " Stitches from Old English Embroideries "
" Stitches from Eastern Embroideries " " Stitches from Western Embroideries "
" Leaves from my Embroidery Book "

WITH A PREFACE BY

REGINALD M. Y. GLEADOWE
Slade Professor of Fine Arts, Oxford University

Embroidery

Embroidery is the handicraft of decorating fabric or other materials with needle and thread or yarn. Embroidery may also incorporate other materials such as metal strips, pearls, beads, quills, and sequins. An interesting characteristic of embroidery is that the basic techniques or stitches on surviving examples of the earliest patterns —chain stitch, buttonhole or blanket stitch, running stitch, satin stitch, cross stitch—remain the fundamental techniques of hand embroidery today.

In *The Art of Embroidery*, written in 1964 by Marie Schuette and Sigrid Muller-Christensen, they noted the 'striking fact that in the development of embroidery ... there are no changes of materials or techniques which can be felt or interpreted as advances from a primitive to a later, more refined stage. On the other hand, we often find in early works a technical accomplishment and high standard of craftsmanship rarely attained in later times.' Embroidery has been dated to the Warring States period in China (5th-3rd century BC). The process used to tailor, patch, mend and reinforce cloth fostered the development of sewing techniques, and the decorative possibilities of sewing led to the art of embroidery. Embroidery was also a very important art in the Medieval Islamic world. One of the most interesting accounts of the craft has been given by the seventeenth century Turkish traveller, Evliya Çelebi, who called it the 'craft of the two hands.'

Because embroidery was a sign of high social status in Muslim societies, it became a hugely popular art. In cities such as Damascus, Cairo and Istanbul, embroidery was visible on handkerchiefs, uniforms, flags, horse trappings, slippers, sheaths, covers, and even on leather belts; often utilising gold and silver thread. It has since spread to the rest of the world, particularly the UK, where professional workshops and guilds garnered an immense reputation. The output of these workshops, called *Opus Anglicanum* or 'English work', was famous throughout Europe.

Embroidery can be classified according to whether the design is stitched *on top of* or *through* the foundation fabric, and by the relationship of stitch placement to the fabric. Several important classifications include 'free embroidery', where designs are applied without regard to the weave of the underlying fabric (such as traditional Chinese and Japanese embroidery), 'Counted Thread embroidery' where patterns are created by making stitches over a predetermined number of threads in the foundation fabric, and 'Canvas Work', where threads are stitched through a fabric mesh to create a dense pattern that completely covers the foundation fabric. This can be done on almost any fabric; wool, linen and silk have been in use for thousands of years, although today - cotton, ribbons, and organza are frequently utilised.

Whilst there is now a burgeoning market for commercial embroidery, and much contemporary embroidery is stitched with a computer using digital patterns, the art and pleasure of embroidery as a craft is making a comeback. We hope that the reader is inspired by this book to try some of their own!

PREFACE

ONE of the ways in which civilised man, the victim of boredom, machinery, mass-production and standardised culture, tries to recapture something of the zest of a more primitive life of personal achievement, is in the making with his own hands of beautiful things. The skill required for such work is often slight; and dexterity has not yet ceased to be the birthright of the race. But the ability to make a thing which is not only a " good job " but also beautiful is a rarer gift, and much first-rate craftsmanship goes to the making of objects which, for poverty or imperfection of design, fail to achieve beauty. Of no craft is this more true than of Embroidery.

Design for Embroidery is a question of both form and colour; the traditional sense of which has, in the main, been lost. Of the two, a sense of colour seems the more common survival. Most embroiderers would feel helpless if they set out to invent anything but the simplest formal pattern; but, given the pattern, they would have ideas—and perhaps good ideas—about the colour.

Miss Pesel's admirable handbooks on various traditional stitches come to the assistance of the worker exactly where, in the matter of formal design, he (or she) is weakest. Believing that there is a national or racial character which expresses itself in design, she argues that English workers will take more kindly to a recovered English tradition than to a Turkish or Norwegian.

She knows the tradition intimately; and she explains in simple terms its principles and some of its motives. There is thus placed into the hand of the embroiderer who rightly wishes to design her (or his) own work an easy means of making a good start by arranging traditional motives on principles which have succeeded in the past.

But the method is not slavish; it has in it the seeds of its own development into an unfettered freedom; so that, starting from this beginning, the designer will be able, according to her gifts, to invent whatever pleases her fancy or suits her skill.

7

The English tradition of cross-stitch design, which can be studied most easily in number-less samplers, particularly of the seventeenth century, is based on a simplification of obvious and pleasing natural forms into rectangular and square-diagonal forms, the double merit of which is their easy working and the simplicity of their pattern. Such forms lend themselves to an artless symmetry and repetition ; and the beauty of English patterns, even if elaborated, can be seen at a glance. The natural forms are mostly flowers and trees, but abstract forms are used as accessories and sometimes, with excellent effect, for whole designs. The essential of such designing is that it should be done on the square. The strict and orderly convention of the square and true diagonal precludes an undue degree of " realism " in interpreting Nature, secures a marked and lively rhythm, and itself helps the imagination to invent motives suitable for a diagonal technique. It will be found that children who on plain paper could do nothing, can usually make a good pattern on square paper.

As to colour Miss Pesel lays down no principles (in other volumes she recommends the range found in good Oriental rugs) ; and there seems some reason to agree with her that, left to herself, even the simplest worker will not be at a loss to colour a good design.

The writer of this book is no theorist. Her opinions are based on much experience of working, organising and teaching. Certainly the fine work done by others under her direc-tion—particularly the Wolvesey Embroidery Guild and the Twyford Women's Institute—show how the application of the right principles for only a short time can help the average worker to enrich the world with well-made things of quiet and lasting beauty. And those who ponder the significance of the movement in which Miss Pesel is taking a leading part will hope that it may not be long before many British children will be making their samplers, and many British women at work on masterpieces.

R. GLEADOWE.

February 1931

8

ACKNOWLEDGMENTS

I GIVE my grateful thanks for permission to make drawings, in order to illustrate yet THANKS. another volume on English Embroidery.

My thanks are due to the authorities of the Victoria and Albert Museum for their unfailing kindness to me. To Mrs. Longman, who has allowed me to use one of her samplers as a coloured frontispiece, and for Plate I. To Lady Egerton and Mrs. Clement Williams, who are owners of some beautiful old specimens of seventeenth-century work.

The Bishop of Winchester kindly allowed me to photograph some of the cushions and kneelers which had been worked, on these designs, for Wolvesey private chapel; and Miss Rooke gave permission to reproduce the carpet worked by the Twyford Group of Women's Institutes, in order to show how little the joining of sections of cross-stitch show when they are completed carefully.

CONTENTS & LIST OF PLATES

11

PLATE I.

UPPER HALF
* See Plate IX. No. 9.

LOWER HALF
* See *Practical Canvas Embroidery*, Plate VII. No. 28

ENGLISH SAMPLER OF SUSANNA INGRAM, 1700
(Size 11 inches by 8¾ inches)

In the possession of MRS. LONGMAN.

PLATE II.

XVI. (26)

XI. (A)

UPPER HALF

XIV. (17)

XIII. (16)

LOWER HALF

XV. 21

ENGLISH SAMPLER
(Size 34⅜ inches by 6¾ inches)
The figures at the sides indicate references to Plates illustrating diagrams showing practical methods of working.

From the Collection of LADY EGERTON.

INTRODUCTION

WITH many workers Cross-Stitch always has been and always will be a favourite stitch, because the beautiful effects to be obtained by the use of this very simple and easy stitch are so many and varied. The texture of the work depends on the size and quality of the stitch and the regularity of the workmanship. It can be very fine and delicate, or coarse and bold, according to its purpose. Then, again, it is modified by the materials on which and in which it is worked—fine linen or coarse canvas, silks or wools. These are matters of personal taste.

What, however, is more important than any of these, is the design—that it should be good and suitable to its use. Now, whereas a novice and amateur can generally procure the right materials and with practice can arrive at a good technique, she cannot always quite so easily get good designs. As I urged in my previous volume on English Embroidery, *Double-running or Back-Stitch*, I feel personally that we should try to secure British designs on which to rebuild a national tradition in embroidery. I have therefore collected and drawn out a number of the simple cross-stitch patterns that are to be found on the old English samplers, as they contain certain elements which reflect our character—elements not found so suitably for us in, say, Italian or Russian work.

The makers of these old samplers were British, and they worked them from our point of view. It is therefore probable—I had almost said certain—that we, in using them again, with our own personal modifications added, shall be able to produce work with a more definitely national character than if we copied models which had, in the first instance, been worked by embroiderers of another nationality.

Turn over a book of coloured illustrations of Swedish, Danish, or Italian embroideries as I have done recently, and you will feel that interesting and beautiful as they undoubtedly are, they are not just the effects, either of colour or balance, that we here, at home, would have produced.

HOW TO USE THESE DESIGNS.

In preparing these designs, I have always had it in mind that they are only offered as suggestions on which a worker can base her own efforts. The flowers may be modified, the size altered, the width of a scroll changed. They are not necessarily to be the final design, they are to be the starting-point of a new one.

What proves my point, that this is the right way to use designs, is the fact that even in the few illustrations given, it will be seen that my drawings are not always exactly like the same design in the photographs of the samplers. In one case I found the same design on six or eight different samplers, all just a little different in some small detail, this variation occurring because each worker had adapted it to suit her own taste and needs. For example, the design of carnations united by an interlaced scroll is different on the sampler worked by Susanna Ingram (1700) and on the coloured reproduction, and I gave a third variation in *Practical Canvas Embroidery.*

Another suggestion as to the possible use of these designs, is that a detail or flower in a border can be taken as the unit of a design and developed into a square or octagonal shape. This is shown in some of the photographs of the Wolvesey cushions, the designs for them being built up from units in these cross-stitch borders.

The octagonal litany stool was covered with a design made up from the carnation design referred to above.

TECHNIQUE.

DIAGRAMS of stitches and details about them were given in *Practical Canvas Embroidery,* and so need not be repeated again. Two stitches given there (C, Fig. 1, and G, Fig. 2) were very commonly used on these old English samplers.

C, a " seventeenth-century diagonal cross-stitch with a bar," over 2, 4, or 6 threads, is the way in which all heavy diagonals were worked. At first it seems a difficult stitch to follow, but it is soon mastered, and then is found to be a most accommodating one to work, as it fulfils all requirements so exceptionally well.

G, " English seventeenth-century cross-stitch with a bar," is used for all the heavier outlines, and it too is an adaptable stitch and, worked with C, seems to fill its purpose admirably.

These patterns can be worked in outline on linen, or if worked on canvas the background can be filled in either in long-legged cross-stitch (F, Fig. 2), or in (A, Fig. 1), gros-point.

PLATE III.

LOWER HALF   * See Plate XIV. No. 19.

In the possession of Mrs. CLEMENT WILLIAMS.

ENGLISH SAMPLER
(Size 21 inches by 6 inches)

UPPER HALF

CARPET WORKED BY TWYFORD GROUP OF WOMEN'S INSTITUTES (HANTS)

MATERIALS . . Wool on coarse Penelope canvas.
COLOURS . . Blues, reds, greens, yellow, camel, and some nigger.
STITCH . . Diagonal cross-stitch (*Canvas Embroidery*, Fig. 1, A 2).
DESIGN . . From an old carpet in the Victoria and Albert Museum.

Lent by MISS ROOKE.

PLATE IV.

Worked on canvas, they would be suitable for a cover for a president's table for a Women's Institute, and could be worked co-operatively. The borders could be done in sections and joined, and the top could also be worked in separate portions, and all finally joined together. Wools and a coarse canvas would be the most suitable materials for such a purpose.

Many of these designs would be suitable for a co-operative gift to a village church. A simple frontal, dossal curtains, kneelers, and alms-bags could all be planned from units in these drawings.

Turning to quite a different type of embroidery, they could be used on a linen with threads withdrawn and over-sewn to give an open background, and the pattern darned in again with a heavier linen ; and would be suitable in this form for borders for short white linen curtains, as the pattern would tell against the light.

IT will perhaps make the drawings easier to understand if one is explained in detail, as they are all prepared on the same plan.

Take No. 26. The line of squares on the diagonal represents, in the original, a line worked in C, seventeenth-century diagonal cross-stitch with bar. It could, of course, be worked in ordinary cross-stitch, but in the original piece this extra thickness was given.

They could also be worked in some square pulled diagonal stitch, if the design was being used for white work.

The lines which are shaded were originally worked in G, but could be worked in long-legged cross-stitch or even in ordinary cross-stitch, or for use for white work in a square open hem-stitch.

The flowers and the leaves could either be left open or filled in, according to the needs of the finished work.

In No. 27 a portion is shaded in, in order to show the weight and effect of the solid masses (however they were worked) as compared with the surrounding line work in double running.

To explain how these designs can be taken as suggestions, examine No. 6, for example. Take one repeat of the wave, and instead of continuing the wave-line right and left, carry the lines upwards. Raise the position of the flower head, and insert some leaves where the flower is, and there is the foundation for the design of a flat alms-bag. As it now is, very little is left of the original design : only a new use made of the elements it contains.

19

Nos. 13, 14, and 19 could be used for small bags, repeating them to make all-over designs. If a variation is desired, some other detail could be inserted into the centres. The design as it stands might be used as an idea for the general spacing.

Nos. 20 and 27 could be repeated twice, facing right and left for a big handbag, or four times, all radiating from the centre to make a square. The shading in No. 22 is used only to show what should be worked solid.

These explanations are purposely given in a very simple form, as they are intended to help the beginner—the expert not requiring any such aid. They will perhaps make it possible for the novice to attempt work in cross-stitch without further help. If they do this they will have fulfilled their purpose, and I shall be amply repaid for the endless time it has taken to draw them out to scale from photographs and from hurried museum notes. They are, in truth, only working diagrams rather than actual finished drawings, because the originals were often worked most irregularly, and all one could do was to give an impression of the design on which they were based. May they prove an inspiration to many British women to attempt good work, and so revive our national prestige in that very personal art—Embroidery.

LOUISA F. PESEL.

TWYFORD,
Spring, 1931.

PLATE V.

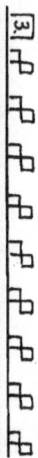

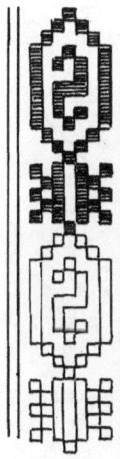

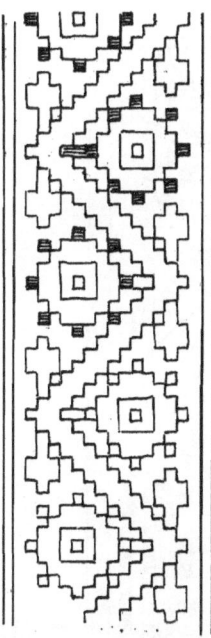

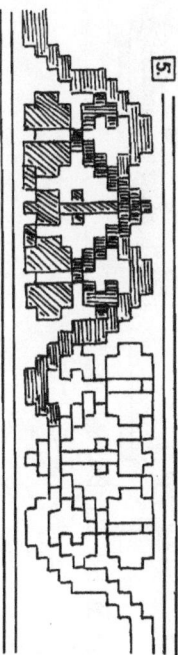

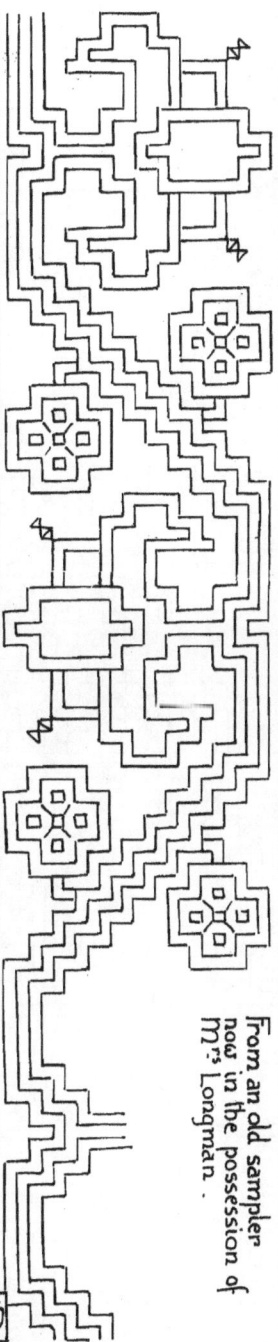

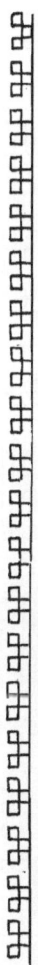

Nᵒˢ 1 to 5 from a sampler. V.v A.M. 829–1902.

From an old sampler now in the possession of Mʳˢ Longman.

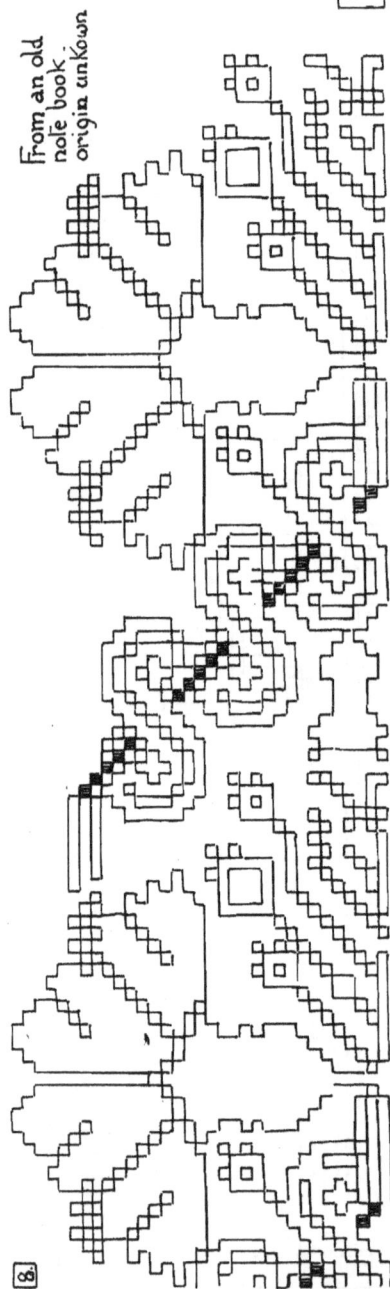

PLATE VI.

[7] a variation of Nº 9 from another sampler.

[8]

From an old
note book,
origin unkown

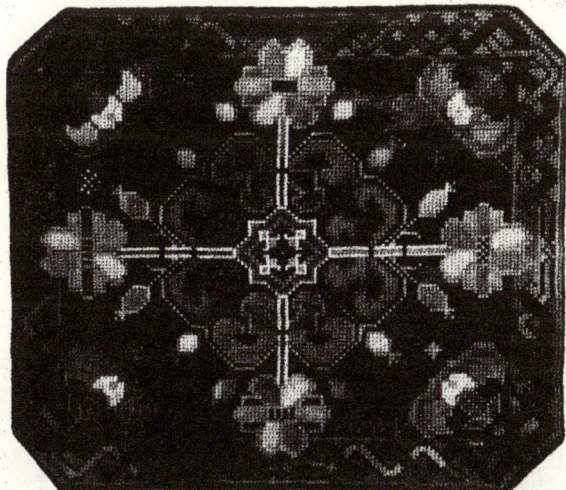

EXAMPLES SHOWING THE USE OF THE SAME DESIGN, BUT REVERSING THE COLOURS

From a set of stall and chair seats and kneelers, worked by the Wolvesey Canvas Embroidery Guild for the Bishop of Winchester's Private Chapel at Wolvesey.

DESIGNS . . Adapted from various seventeenth-century English samplers.

MATERIALS . . Wools and a coarse single open hemp canvas.

COLOURS . . Vary in different designs, but are mainly either blues and yellow or reds, blues, and greens, with either cream and buff, or deep wine colour as a background.

STITCHES . . Long-legged cross-stitch was used throughout the whole set, this type of treatment having been suggested by the Spanish carpet illustrated as the frontispiece in *Practical Canvas Embroidery*.

See Plate No. 29 XVII, ; also Frontispiece.

PLATE VII.

A

B

PLATE VIII.

(A) Notecase and (B) Pochette
Worked by the Author

(A) Design . . . Suggested by spacing on a rug.
MATERIALS . . Wools on fine canvas.
COLOURS . . Deep reds, blues, and some nigger.
STITCHES . . Pattern: long-legged cross-stitch. Grounding: in tent or cushion stitch.

(See *Eastern Samplers*, by L. F. Pesel. Plate 62A.)

(B) DESIGN . . . Adapted from border, Plate I., also Plate VI.
MATERIALS . . Wools and a little silk on fine single canvas.
COLOURS . . Mainly blues and greens on a red ground.
STITCHES . . Petit point (see *Canvas Embroidery*, Fig. 1 B. English Long-legged Cross-Stitch with Bar, Fig. 2 G. English Diagonal Cross-Stitch with Bar, Fig. 1 C. See Plate IX., No. 9.

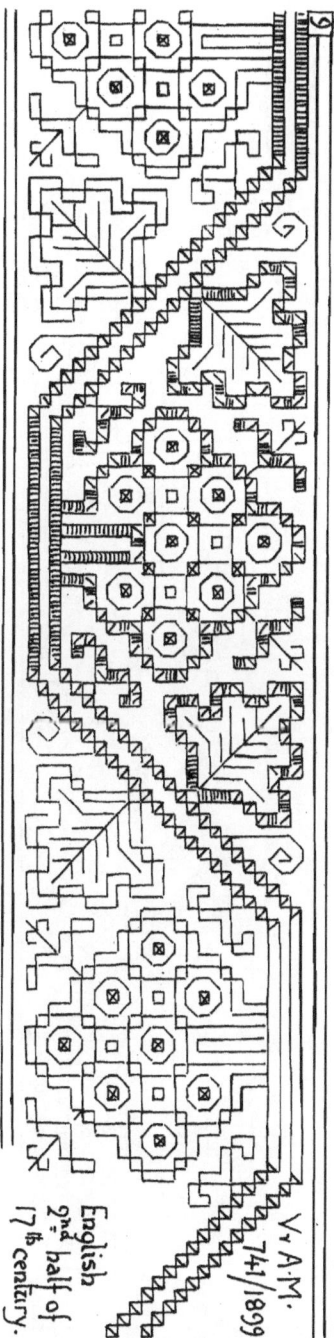

PLATE IX.

V. A. M.
741/1899

English
2nd half of
17th century.

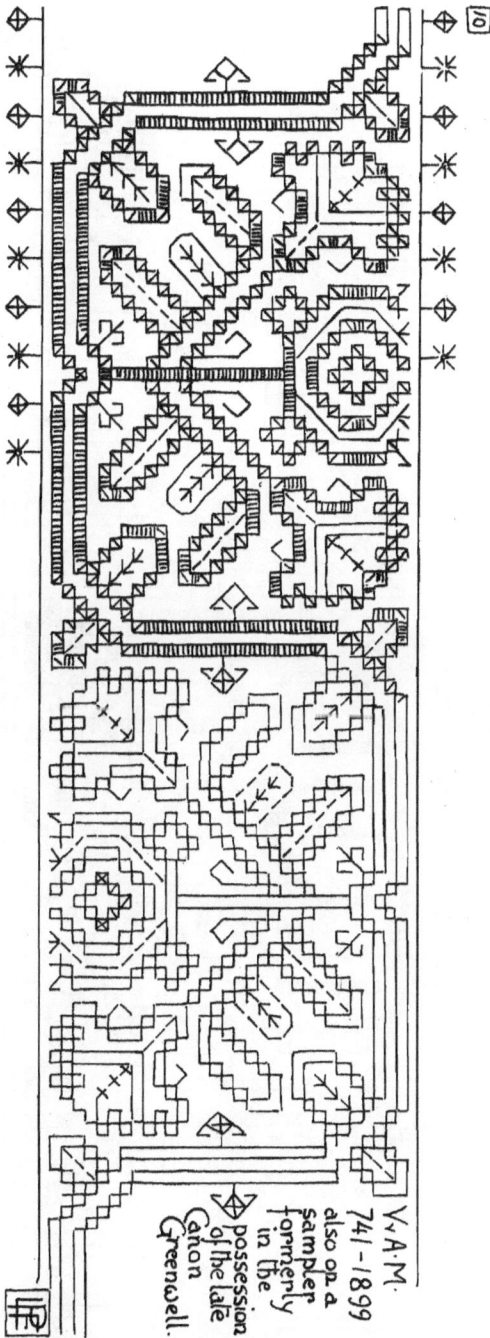

V. A. M.
741-1899
also on a
sampler
formerly
in the
possession
of the late
Canon
Greenwell.

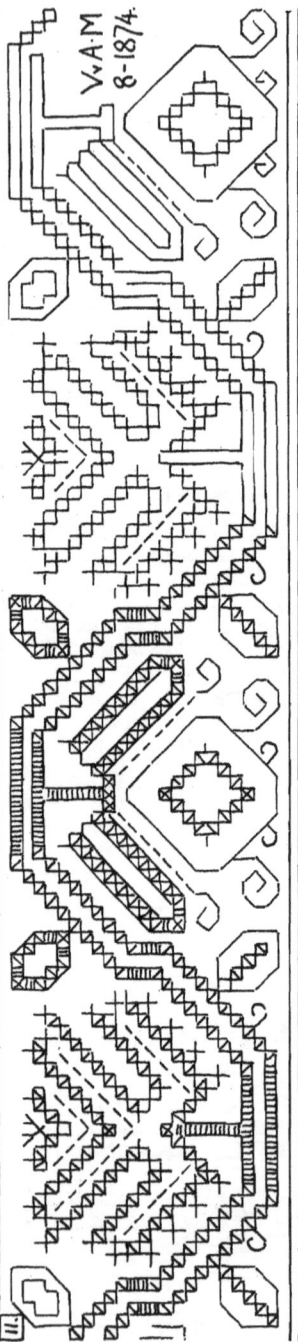

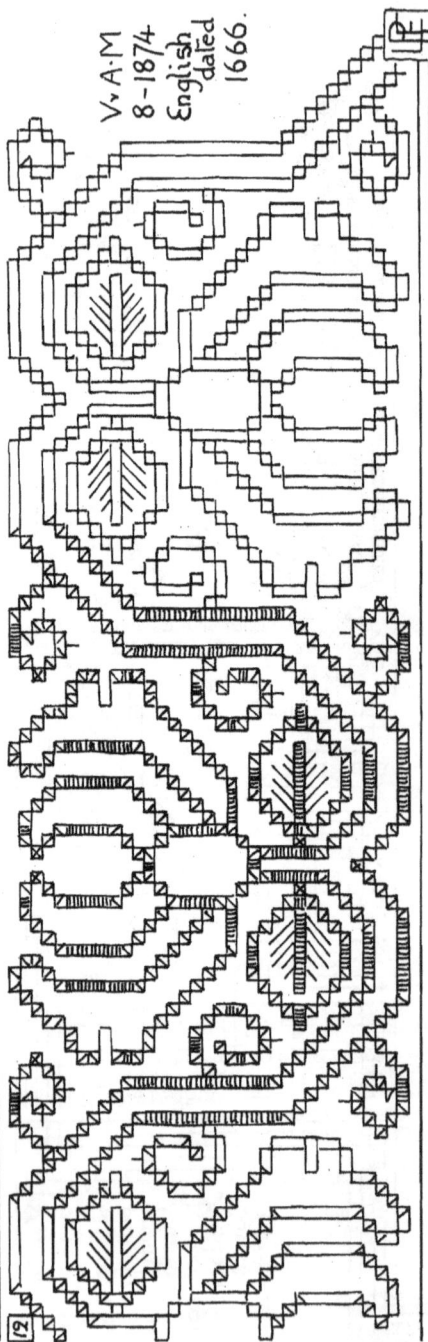

PLATE X.

V·A·M
8-1874.

V·A·M
8-1874.
English
dated
1666.

A

Example from the Set of Stall and Chair Seats and Kneelers
Worked by the Wolvesey Canvas Embroidery Guild for the Bishop
of Winchester's Private Chapel at Wolvesey.

See Plate II. *1, and Plate X. No. 12.

B

A Stall Cushion
From the Wolvesey Set

PLATE XI.

PLATE XII.

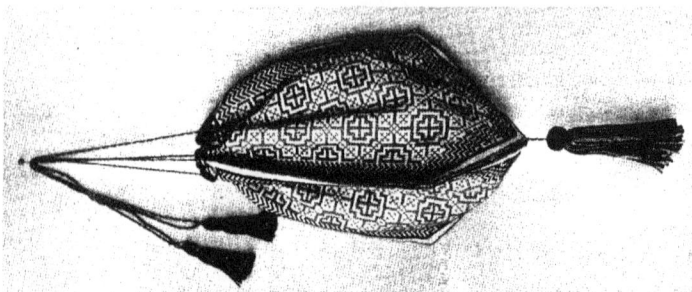

SMALL WORK-BAG
Worked by Mrs. STUBBINGTON

MATERIALS . : D.M.C. cottons on a linen ground.
COLOURS : Blue and nigger.
STITCHES : Cross-stitch, long-legged cross-stitch, surface darning for the borders.
DESIGN . : From a seventeenth-century sampler.

See
Plate XIII.,
Figs. 14 & 15.
Similar
designs,
Plate XIV.,
No. 19.

ANOTHER EXAMPLE FROM THE SET OF STALL AND CHAIR SEATS AND KNEELERS.
Worked by the Wolvesey Canvas Embroidery Guild for the Bishop of Winchester's Private
Chapel at Wolvesey

13 V·A·M·516-1877.

14 V·A·M· 266 1911.

solid

solid

solid

PLATE XIII.

15

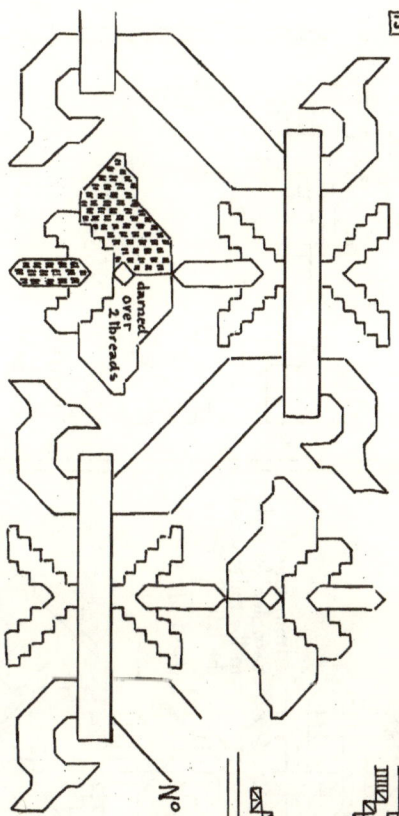

damned over 2 threads

16

Nº 15 From a sampler in the possession of Mrs Clement Williams

V·A·M·804-1877

The curved band could be made 2 squares narrower & the flowers 2 squares wider if big spaces were required for pulled fillings.

PLATE XIV.

V·A·M 266 – 1911
English
2ⁿᵈ half 17ᵗʰ century.

solid.

solid.

Formerly
in the late
Mʳˢ Crolys
collection

English
17ᵗʰ century

17

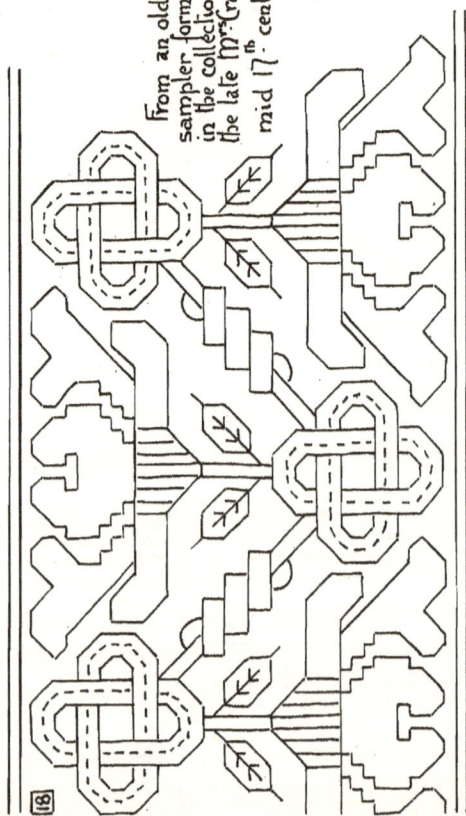

From an old
sampler formerly
in the collection of
the late Mʳˢ Croly.
mid 17ᵗʰ century

18

19

20 V·A·M· 804/1877.

dated 1656

22

V·A·M· 368/1907.
English
dated 1661.

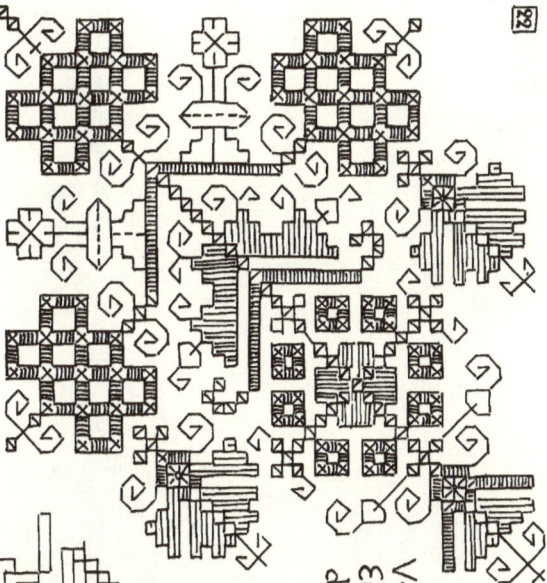

21

V·A·M· 829-1902.

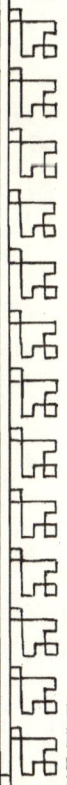

PLATE XV.

V·A·M· 741-1899

23

PLATE XVI.

V·A·M·804 - 1877

25

V·A·M 368-1907. dated 1661.

27

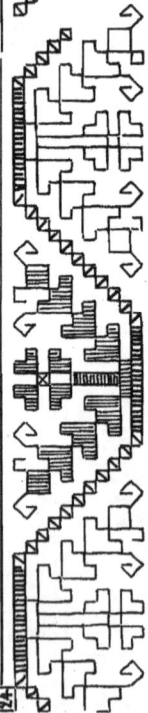

V·A·M. 829 - 1902

26

English
V·A·M.
829-1902

28   V·A·M 17ᵗʰ century English.

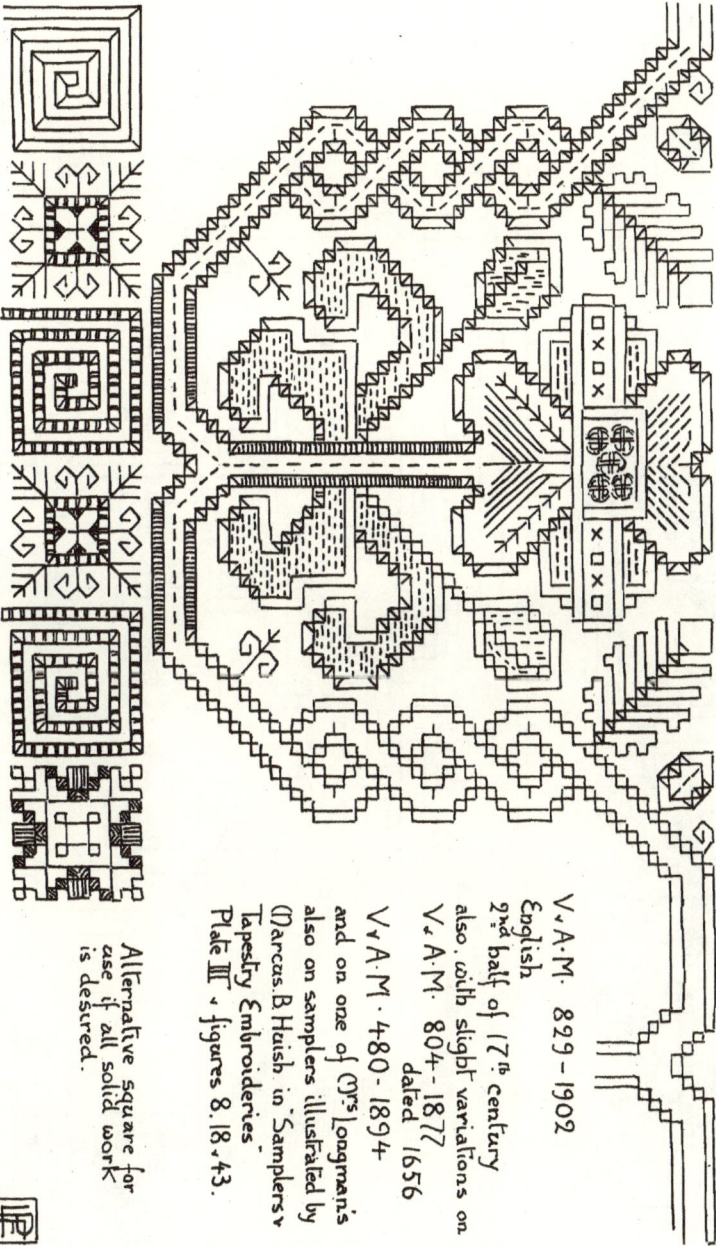

V·A·M· 829-1902
English
2ⁿᵈ half of 17ᵗʰ century
also, with slight variations on
V·A·M· 804-1877
dated 1656

V·A·M· 480-1894
and on one of Mʳˢ Longman's
also on samplers illustrated by
Marcus B. Huish in "Samplers v
Tapestry Embroideries"
Plate III, figures 8.18,43.

Alternative square for
use if all solid work
is desired.

PLATE XVII.

PLATE XVIII.

31

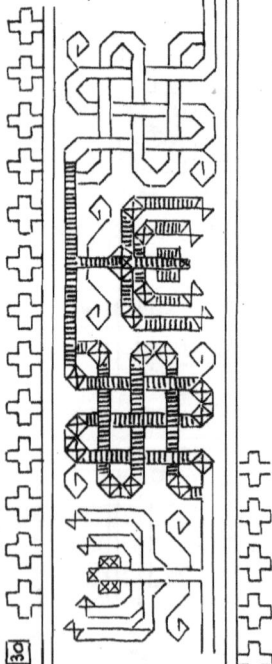

Nos 30, 32 from a
sampler in the
possession of
(M)rs Longman

English
second half of
17th century

30

32

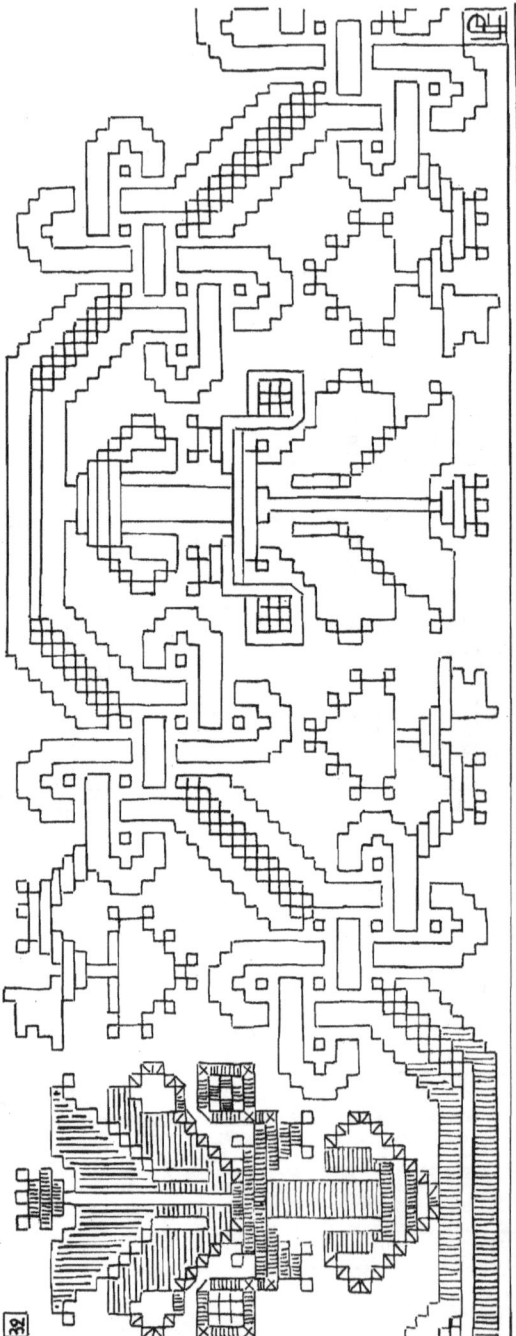

NOTES

NOTES